Life After Graduation

ISBN: 1-57051-765-7

Illustrations:
Alison Jerry

Cover/Interior Design:
Koechel Peterson & Associates, Minneapolis, MN

Concept/Art Direction:
Joanne Fink

Printed in USA

A Special Gift

For
my favorite Nephew
(one of them)

With Love From
Auntie Terri

Date
May 29,03

I'm very Proud of You !!

xo

Table of Contents

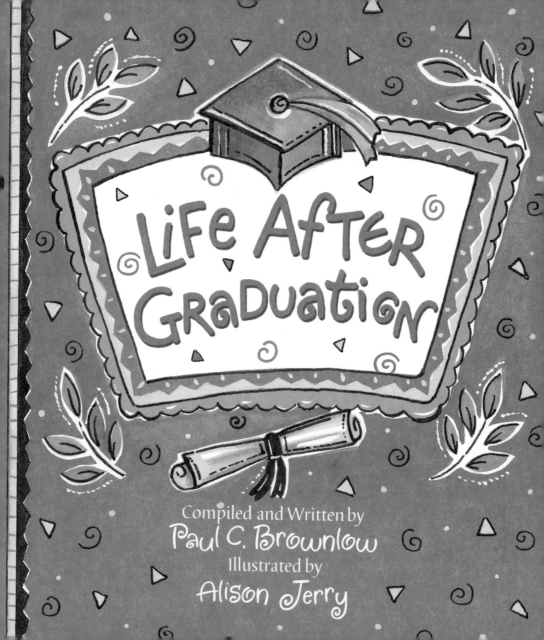

LiFe AFTER GRaDuATioN

Compiled and Written by
Paul C. Brownlow

Illustrated by
Alison Jerry

CHAPTER ONE

Friends Are Like Peanut Butter

Friends are like Peanut Butter.

They come in two varieties—Regular and Extra Crunchy.

Try to stock up on both kinds.

Regular friends are good everyday.

But the Extra Crunchy friends add

that special burst of flavor to everything.

Paul C. Brownlow

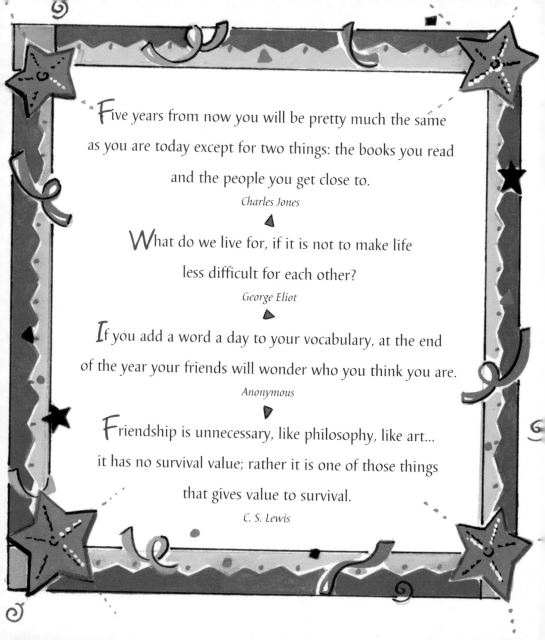

Five years from now you will be pretty much the same
as you are today except for two things: the books you read
and the people you get close to.

Charles Jones

What do we live for, if it is not to make life
less difficult for each other?

George Eliot

If you add a word a day to your vocabulary, at the end
of the year your friends will wonder who you think you are.

Anonymous

Friendship is unnecessary, like philosophy, like art...
it has no survival value; rather it is one of those things
that gives value to survival.

C. S. Lewis

Anyone with a heart full of friendship has a hard time finding enemies.

Anonymous

Sowing seeds of peace is like sowing beans.

You don't know why it works;

you just know it does.

Max Lucado

▶

What a pity that so many people are living with

so few friends when the world is full

of lonesome strangers who would give anything

just to be somebody's friend.

Mike L. Arnold

◀

Be kind and compassionate to one another,

forgiving each other, just as in Christ God forgave you.

Ephesians 4:32

◀

A friend is one who makes me do my best.

Oswald Chambers

CHAPTER TWO

Who Do You Want to Be When You Grow Up?

Growing up means choosing to meet
someone else's need rather than your own.

Anonymous

More depends on my walk than my talk.

D. L. Moody

*Y*ou will have to make a lot of important decisions,
even though most of them may seem small at the time.
It will not be nearly so hard to make them if you remember
who you are and what your values are.

Paul C. Brownlow

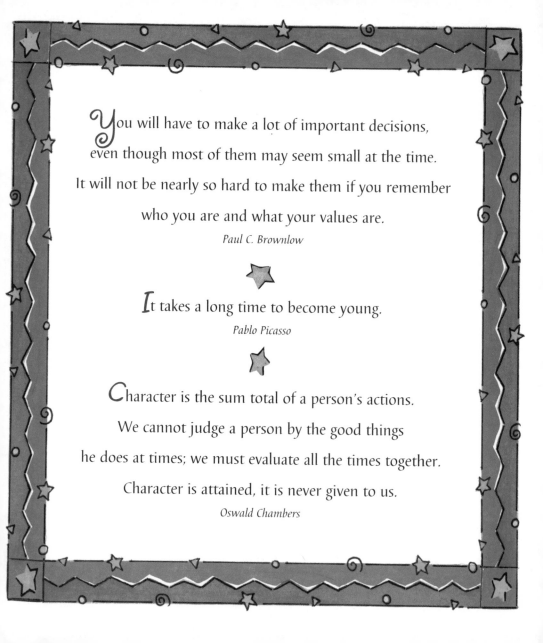

*I*t takes a long time to become young.

Pablo Picasso

*C*haracter is the sum total of a person's actions.
We cannot judge a person by the good things
he does at times; we must evaluate all the times together.
Character is attained, it is never given to us.

Oswald Chambers

Don't worship the crowd, your peers, your friends.

Expressing your individuality by dressing

just like everyone else may not be so bad.

But there will be a time when you will have to say "No."

Have the courage to be different.

Paul C. Brownlow

Perseverance must finish its work

so that you may be mature and complete,

not lacking anything.

James 1:4

Character is always lost when a high ideal is sacrificed on

the altar of conformity and popularity.

Chuck Swindoll

There is no danger of developing eye strain from looking on the bright side of life.

CHAPTER THREE

Proverbs Solomon Didn't Write— But They're Still Pretty Good

Life is like an onion; you peel off

one layer at a time and sometimes you weep.

Carl Sandburg

Sometimes life is like dancing with a gorilla:

You're not done until the gorilla is.

Anonymous

To travel hopefully is a better thing than to arrive.

Robert Louis Stevenson

Happiness is a thing to be practiced, like the violin.

John Lubbock

Learn to think for yourself.

You are not everybody's dog that whistles.

Early American Proverb

All degrees of joy reside in the heart.

Oswald Chambers

The great tragedy of life is not that men perish,

but that they cease to love.

W. Somerset Maugham

Laughter is the shortest distance between people.

Victor Borge

God gave man the ability to forget, which is one of

the greatest attributes. People who go around

"keeping score" are miserable people.

Hubert H. Humphrey

Too many folks go through life running

from something that isn't after them.

Anonymous

Worry does not empty tomorrow of its sorrow;

it empties today of its strength.

Corrie Ten Boom

*Y*esterday is history, tomorrow is a mystery,
and today is a gift; that's why they call it the present.

*N*o clever arrangement of bad eggs

ever made a good omelet.

C. S. Lewis

*D*on't tell me that worry doesn't do any good.

Most of the things I worry about don't happen.

Anonymous

I avoid looking forward or backward,

and try to keep looking upward.

Charlotte Brontë

*D*on't expect your neighbor to be better

than your neighbor's neighbor.

Anonymous

CHAPTER FOUR

Family Peace and Two T.V.'s

Keeping peace in the family requires

patience, love, understanding, and at least two TV sets.

Anonymous

The family you come from isn't as important

as the family you're going to have.

Ring Lardner

Ninety percent of the friction of daily life

is caused by the wrong tone of voice.

Anonymous

Marriage is for love, for friendship, for a lifetime.

A great wedding does not make a great marriage.

Great marriages must be made and remade daily.

Paul C. Brownlow

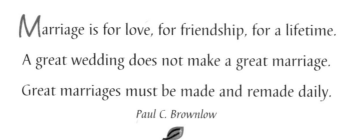

Being married teaches us at least one very valuable lesson—

to think before we speak.

Anonymous

What right have I to make every one in the house

miserable because I am miserable? Troubles must come

to all, but troubles need not be wicked,

and it is wicked to be a destroyer of happiness.

Amelia E. Barr

Success in marriage is more than finding the right person;

it is a matter of being the right person.

Anonymous

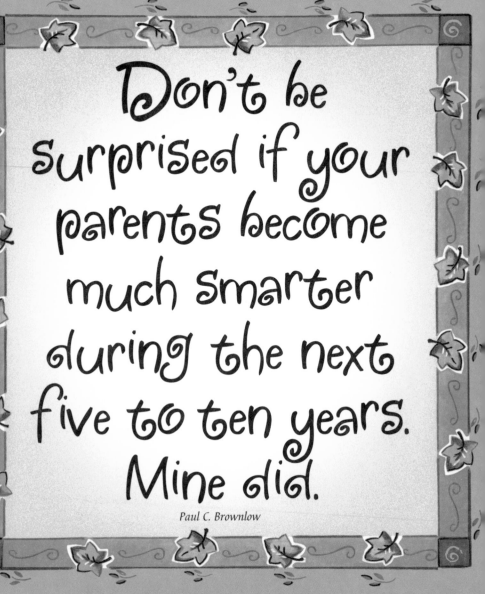

Don't be surprised if your parents become much smarter during the next five to ten years. Mine did.

Paul C. Brownlow

Spare the rod and spoil the child—that is true. But,
beside the rod, keep an apple to give him when he has done well.

Martin Luther

Anyone can build a house: we need the Lord

for the creation of a home.

John Henry Jowett

Call it a clan, call it a network, call it a tribe, call it a family.

Whatever you call it, whoever you are, you need one.

Jane Howard

The Bible does not say very much about homes;

it says a great deal about the things that make them.

It speaks about life and love and joy and peace and rest!

If we get a house and put these into it,

we shall have secured a home.

John Henry Jowett

CHAPTER FIVE

No Shortcuts to Any Place Worth Going

The real voyage of discovery consists not in seeking

new landscapes, but in having new eyes.

Marcel Proust

There are no shortcuts to any place worth going.

Anonymous

Delight yourself in the Lord and he
will give you the desires of your heart.
Psalm 37:4

I am not afraid of tomorrow for I
have seen yesterday and I love today.
William Allen White

Life has meaning,
only as one barters it day by day
for something other than itself.
Antoine de Saint Exupéry

Whatever your past, you have a spotless future.
Anonymous

The really happy people are the ones who can enjoy the scenery even when they have to take a detour.

Those who have a "why" to live,

can bear with almost any "how."

Victor Frankel

Therefore as God's chosen people,

holy and dearly loved, clothe yourself with compassion,

kindness, humility, gentleness and patience.

Colossians 3:12

We should all be concerned about the future because

we have to spend the rest of our lives there.

Charles Kittering

I like the dreams of the future better

than the history of the past.

Thomas Jefferson

God does not want us to do extraordinary things;
he want us to do the ordinary things extraordinarily well.

Charles Gore

Make it a rule of life never to regret

and never to look back. Regret is an

appalling waste of energy; you can't build on it.

Katherine Mansfield

Sow a thought, reap an act;

sow an act, reap a habit;

sow a habit, reap a character;

sow a character, reap a destiny.

Anonymous

CHAPTER SIX

Prayer and HOLY Chewing Gum

A prayer is not holy chewing gum and you don't

have to see how far you can stretch it.

Lionel Blue

Trust in the Lord with all your heart and lean not on your

own understanding; in all your ways acknowledge him,

and he will make your paths straight.

Proverbs 3:5

Believe in the sun, even when it does not shine.

Believe in love, even when you do not feel it.

Believe in God, even when you do not see Him.

Hans Kung (Adapted)

I am often glad that certain prayers

of my past were not granted.

C. S. Lewis

The Bible is meant to be bread for our daily use,

not just cake for special occasions.

Proverb

I used to ask God to help me.

Then I asked if I might help him.

I ended up asking him to do his work through me.

James Hudson Taylor

*D*ear God, help me get up; I can fall down by myself.

Anonymous

*B*ible study is like eating fish. When you find a bone,

you need not throw away the whole fish.

Lay aside the bone and keep eating.

Alex Wilson

*I*t's good to spend time with God every day.

Call home and talk to your Father.

Read the letter He wrote to you.

Paul C. Brownlow

A Bible in the hand is worth two in the bookshelf.

Anonymous

An atheist is a person with no invisible means of support.

Anonymous

When men cease to wonder,

God's secrets remain unrevealed.

Anonymous

Ask, and it shall be given to you; seek,

and you will find; knock, and it shall be opened to you.

Matthew 7:7

Never make the blunder of trying to forecast the way

God is going to answer your prayer.

Oswald Chambers

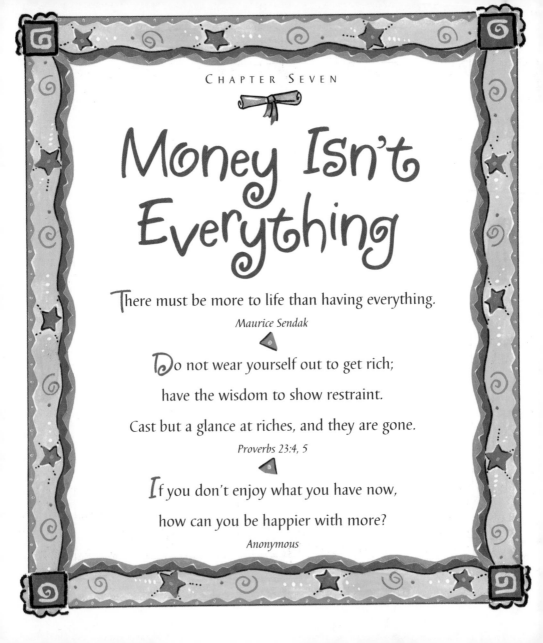

CHAPTER SEVEN

Money Isn't Everything

There must be more to life than having everything.

Maurice Sendak

Do not wear yourself out to get rich;

have the wisdom to show restraint.

Cast but a glance at riches, and they are gone.

Proverbs 23:4, 5

If you don't enjoy what you have now,

how can you be happier with more?

Anonymous

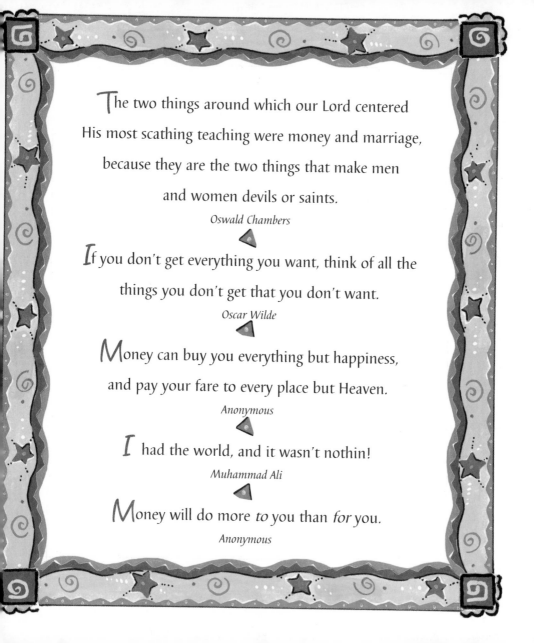

The two things around which our Lord centered His most scathing teaching were money and marriage, because they are the two things that make men and women devils or saints.

Oswald Chambers

If you don't get everything you want, think of all the things you don't get that you don't want.

Oscar Wilde

Money can buy you everything but happiness, and pay your fare to every place but Heaven.

Anonymous

I had the world, and it wasn't nothin!

Muhammad Ali

Money will do more *to* you than *for* you.

Anonymous

Do not store up for yourselves treasures on earth,

where moth and rust destroy,

and where thieves break in and steal.

But store up for yourselves treasures in heaven.

Matthew 6:19-20

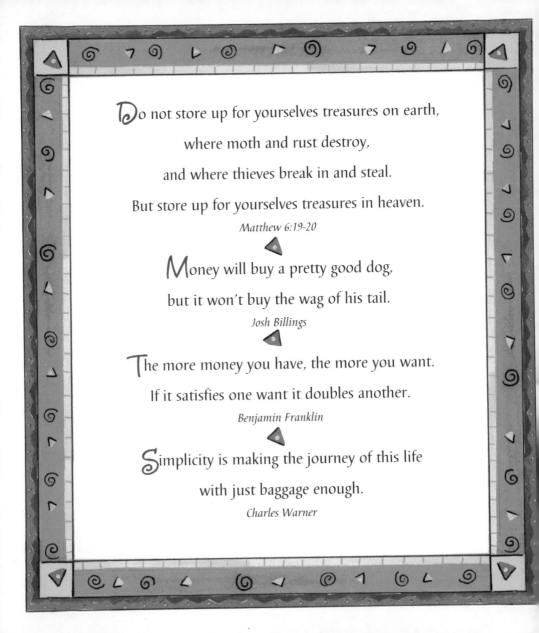

Money will buy a pretty good dog,

but it won't buy the wag of his tail.

Josh Billings

The more money you have, the more you want.

If it satisfies one want it doubles another.

Benjamin Franklin

Simplicity is making the journey of this life

with just baggage enough.

Charles Warner

There was a time
when a fool and
his money were
soon parted.
Now it happens
to everybody.

Anonymous

CHAPTER EIGHT

Life is not Fair

Life is not fair. Anyone who tells you that

is trying to sell something.

Anonymous

The tragedy of life is not that it ends so soon,

but that we wait so long to begin it.

W. M. Lewis

No one grows old by living—

only by losing interest in living.

Marie Benton Ray

There are two things to aim at in life: first, to get what you want; and, after that, to enjoy it. Only the wisest achieve the second.

Logan Pearsall Smith

The second half of a person's life is made up of the habits acquired during the first half.

Fyodor Dostoyevski

Do not love sleep or you will grow poor.

Proverbs 20:13

If you have made mistakes, even serious ones, there is always another chance for you. What we call failure is not the falling down, but the staying down.

Mary Pickford

University of Life

Life is my university,
and I hope to graduate
from it with
some distinction.

Louisa May Alcott

Be glad of life because it gives you the chance to love and to work and to play and to look at the stars.

Henry Van Dyke

A heart at peace gives life to the body.

Proverbs 14:30

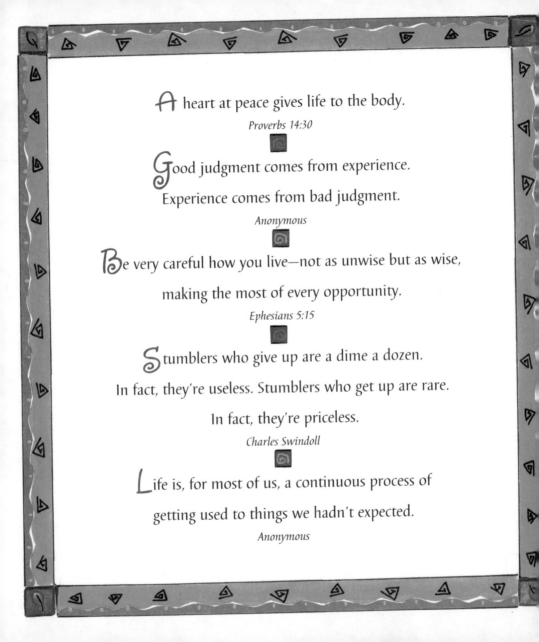

Good judgment comes from experience.

Experience comes from bad judgment.

Anonymous

Be very careful how you live—not as unwise but as wise,

making the most of every opportunity.

Ephesians 5:15

Stumblers who give up are a dime a dozen.

In fact, they're useless. Stumblers who get up are rare.

In fact, they're priceless.

Charles Swindoll

Life is, for most of us, a continuous process of

getting used to things we hadn't expected.

Anonymous

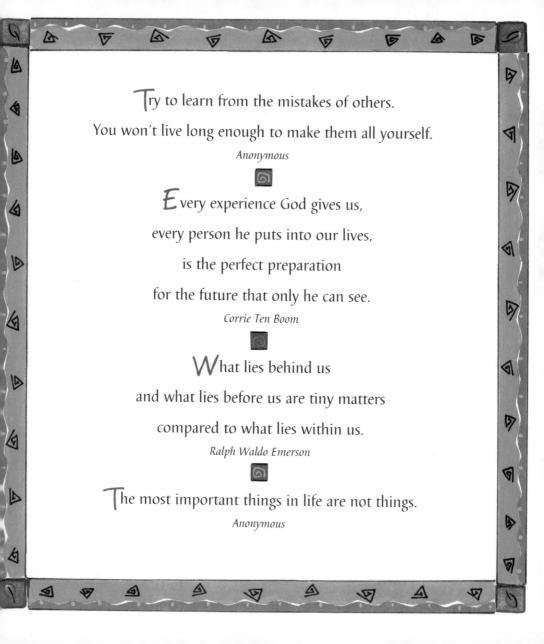

Try to learn from the mistakes of others.

You won't live long enough to make them all yourself.

Anonymous

Every experience God gives us,

every person he puts into our lives,

is the perfect preparation

for the future that only he can see.

Corrie Ten Boom

What lies behind us

and what lies before us are tiny matters

compared to what lies within us.

Ralph Waldo Emerson

The most important things in life are not things.

Anonymous

CHAPTER NINE

Stick With Love

I have decided to stick with love.

Hate is too great a burden to bear.

Martin Luther King, Jr.

*A*s we practice the work of forgiveness,

we discover more and more that forgiveness

and healing are one.

Agnes Sanford

*Y*our love has given me great joy.

Philemon 7

Power can do everything but the most important thing;

it cannot control love.

Philip Yancey

There is only one happiness in life, to love and be loved.

George Sand

Any time that is not spent on love is wasted.

Goethe

When you love someone, you love the whole person,

just as he or she is, and not as you would like them to be.

Leo Tolstoy

There are more people who wish to be loved

than there are willing to love.

S. R. N. Chamfort

*I*t probably would be all right if we'd love

our neighbors as we love ourselves,

but could they stand that much affection?

Anonymous

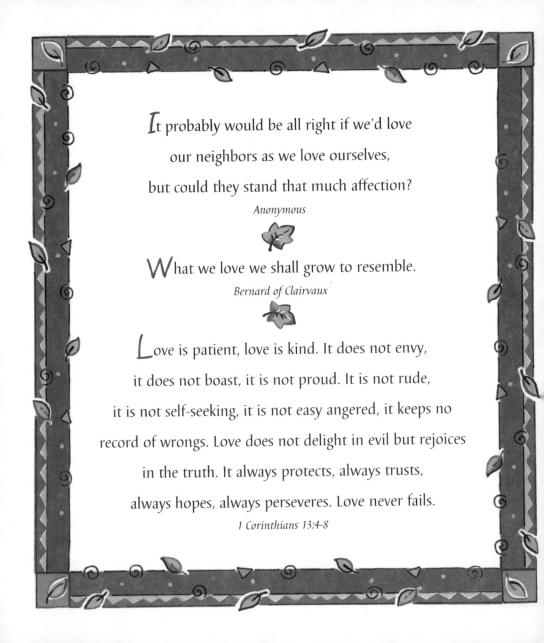

*W*hat we love we shall grow to resemble.

Bernard of Clairvaux

*L*ove is patient, love is kind. It does not envy,

it does not boast, it is not proud. It is not rude,

it is not self-seeking, it is not easy angered, it keeps no

record of wrongs. Love does not delight in evil but rejoices

in the truth. It always protects, always trusts,

always hopes, always perseveres. Love never fails.

1 Corinthians 13:4-8

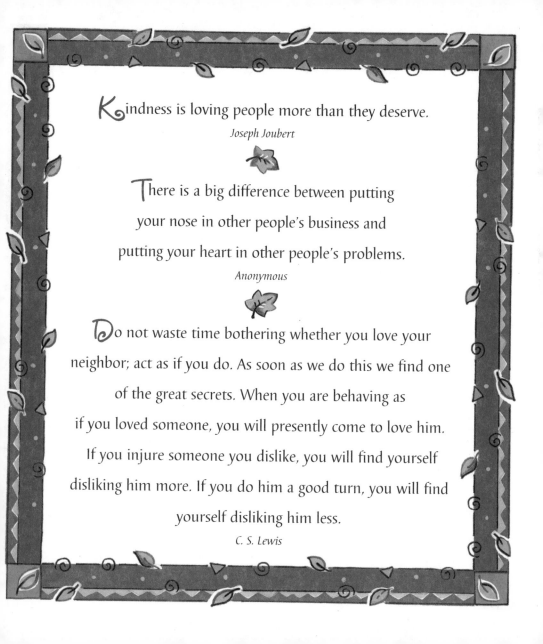

Kindness is loving people more than they deserve.

Joseph Joubert

There is a big difference between putting
your nose in other people's business and
putting your heart in other people's problems.

Anonymous

Do not waste time bothering whether you love your
neighbor; act as if you do. As soon as we do this we find one
of the great secrets. When you are behaving as
if you loved someone, you will presently come to love him.
If you injure someone you dislike, you will find yourself
disliking him more. If you do him a good turn, you will find
yourself disliking him less.

C. S. Lewis

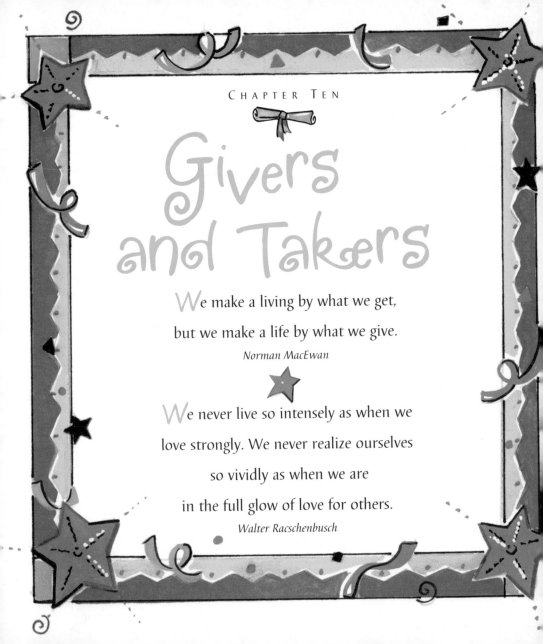

CHAPTER TEN

Givers and Takers

We make a living by what we get,

but we make a life by what we give.

Norman MacEwan

We never live so intensely as when we

love strongly. We never realize ourselves

so vividly as when we are

in the full glow of love for others.

Walter Racschenbusch

When we forget ourselves, we usually do something

that everyone else remembers.

Anonymous

If you have love in your heart, you will always

have something to give.

Anonymous

You can give without loving,

but you cannot love without giving.

Amy Carmichael

If anyone wants to be first, he must be the very last,

and the servant of all.

Mark 9:35

Those who
bring sunshine
to the lives
of others
cannot keep it
from themselves.

James M. Barrie

CHAPTER ELEVEN

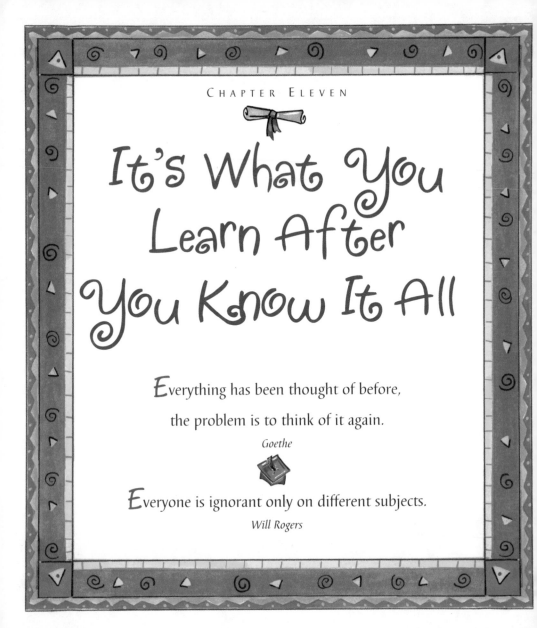

It's What You Learn After You Know It All

Everything has been thought of before,

the problem is to think of it again.

Goethe

Everyone is ignorant only on different subjects.

Will Rogers

The trouble with the world is not that people know so little,

but that they know so many things that ain't so.

Mark Twain

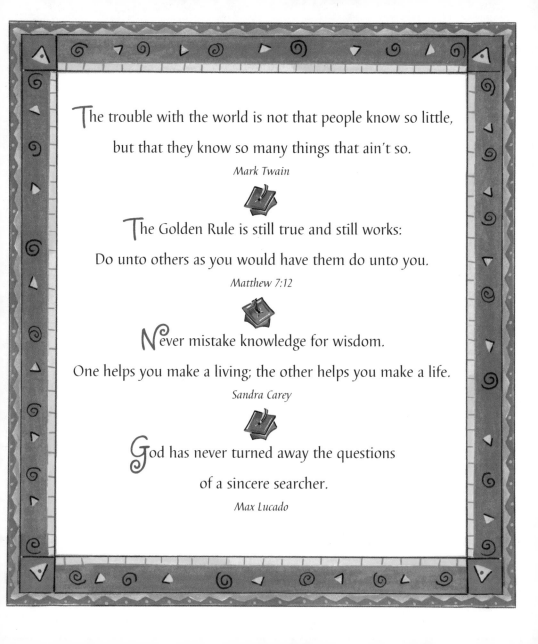

The Golden Rule is still true and still works:

Do unto others as you would have them do unto you.

Matthew 7:12

Never mistake knowledge for wisdom.

One helps you make a living; the other helps you make a life.

Sandra Carey

God has never turned away the questions

of a sincere searcher.

Max Lucado

One can easily recognize a wise person

by the things he does not say.

Anonymous

It's what you learn after you know

it all that really matters.

Proverb

A good listener is not only popular everywhere,

but after awhile he knows something.

Wilson Mizner

You cannot teach a man anything;

you can only help him to find it for himself.

Galileo

For the Lord grants wisdom! His every word is a treasure

of knowledge and understanding.

Proverbs 2:6

Colleges are great reservoirs of knowledge. The freshmen bring in a little every year and the seniors never take any away. And that stuff just naturally accumulates.

Abbott's Journal

CHAPTER TWELVE

Enjoy the Sunshine

Some people are making such thorough preparations

for a rainy day that they aren't enjoying today's sunshine.

There is a big difference between living and

just breathing. Choose to live, not just exist.

Use your gifts and your days wisely,

deliberately. You were put here for a purpose.

Paul C. Brownlow

For the Lord God is a sun and a shield;

the Lord bestows favor and honor; no good thing does

he withhold from those whose walk is blameless.

Psalm 84:11

It is a funny thing about life. If you refuse to accept anything

but the best, you very often get it.

Somerset Maugham

I will not just live my life. I will not just spend my life.

I will invest my life.

Helen Keller

How wonderful it is that nobody need wait a single

moment before starting to improve the world.

Anne Frank

Be a life long or short, its completeness depends

on what it was lived for.

David Starr Jordan

I asked God for all things so I could enjoy life.

He gave me life so I could enjoy all things.

Anonymous

The worst bankrupt person in the world is the one

who has lost his enthusiasm.

H. W. Arnold

Fear not that your life shall come to an end,

but rather fear that it shall never have a beginning.

J. H. Newman

There is nothing new under the sun.

Ecclesiastes 1:9

Worry does not empty tomorrow of its sorrow,

it empties today of its strength.

Corrie Ten Boom

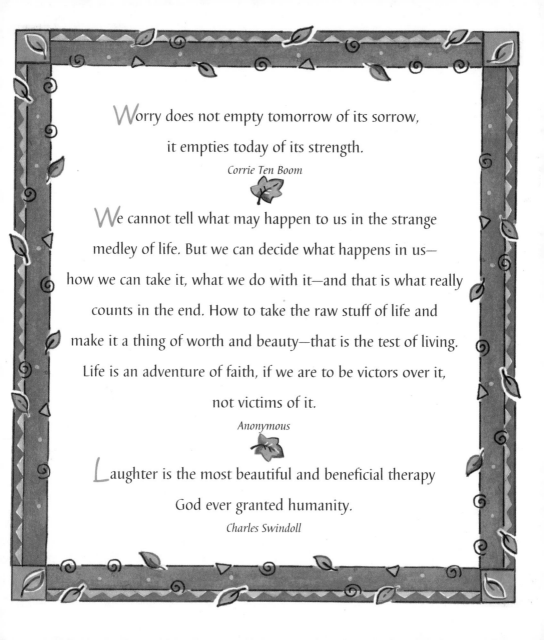

We cannot tell what may happen to us in the strange

medley of life. But we can decide what happens in us—

how we can take it, what we do with it—and that is what really

counts in the end. How to take the raw stuff of life and

make it a thing of worth and beauty—that is the test of living.

Life is an adventure of faith, if we are to be victors over it,

not victims of it.

Anonymous

Laughter is the most beautiful and beneficial therapy

God ever granted humanity.

Charles Swindoll

God's promises are like stars; the darker the night the brighter they shine.

David Nicholas

CHAPTER THIRTEEN

God is Nuts About Us

*G*od loves us the way we are,

but He loves us too much to leave us that way.

Leighton Ford

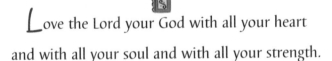

*L*ove the Lord your God with all your heart

and with all your soul and with all your strength.

Deuteronomy 6:5

*O*ur love for God is best tested by the question

of whether we seek him or his gifts.

Ralph Sockman

God doesn't care so much about being analyzed.

Mainly, he wants to be loved.

Philip Yancey

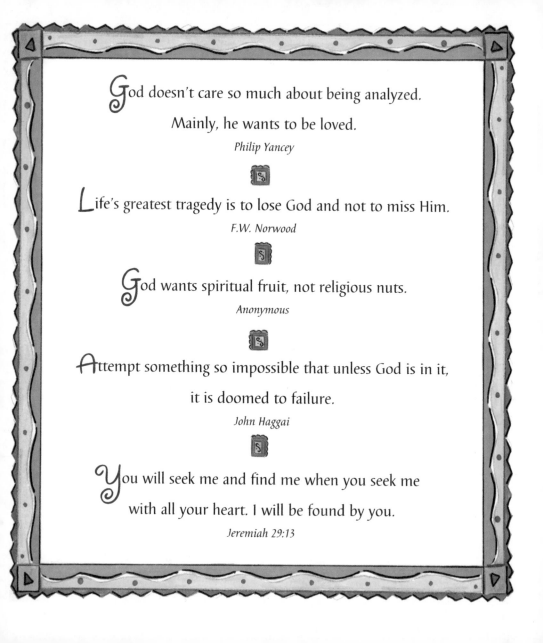

Life's greatest tragedy is to lose God and not to miss Him.

F.W. Norwood

God wants spiritual fruit, not religious nuts.

Anonymous

Attempt something so impossible that unless God is in it,

it is doomed to failure.

John Haggai

You will seek me and find me when you seek me

with all your heart. I will be found by you.

Jeremiah 29:13

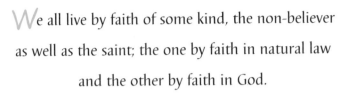

We all live by faith of some kind, the non-believer
as well as the saint; the one by faith in natural law
and the other by faith in God.

A. W. Tozer

We never test the resources of God
until we attempt the impossible.

F. B. Meyer

It's not the passages of the Bible that I don't understand that
give me trouble. It's the ones I understand all too well.

Mark Twain

O Lord, what is man that you care for him,
the son of man that you think of him?

Psalm 144:3

*G*od is nuts about us!
Rick Atchley

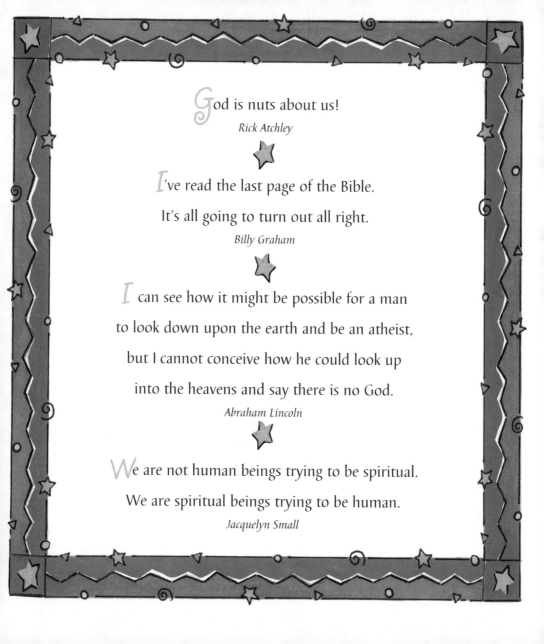

I've read the last page of the Bible.

It's all going to turn out all right.
Billy Graham

I can see how it might be possible for a man

to look down upon the earth and be an atheist,

but I cannot conceive how he could look up

into the heavens and say there is no God.
Abraham Lincoln

*W*e are not human beings trying to be spiritual.

We are spiritual beings trying to be human.
Jacquelyn Small

When you know that God loves you, it helps you love yourself. And when you love yourself, you can love somebody else.

Karl Milton